AYO'S **AWESOME** ADVENTURES

IN

ST. PETERSBURG

CITY OF BRIDGES

WORLD BOOK

www.worldbook.com

World Book, Inc.
180 North LaSalle Street
Suite 900
Chicago, Illinois 60601
USA

For information about other World Book publications, visit our website at www.worldbook.com or call 1-800-WORLDBK (967-5325).

For information about sales to schools and libraries, call 1-800-975-3250 (United States), or 1-800-837-5365 (Canada).

Library of Congress Cataloging-in-Publication Data for this volume has been applied for.

Ayo's Awesome Adventures
ISBN: 978-0-7166-3636-6 (set, hc.)

Ayo's Awesome Adventures in St. Petersburg: City of Bridges
ISBN 978-0-7166-4837-6

Also available as:
ISBN: 978-0-7166-3655-7 (e-book)

1st printing July 2018

Staff

Writer: Jeffrey Osier

Executive Committee

President
Jim O'Rourke

Vice President and
Editor in Chief
Paul A. Kobasa

Vice President, Finance
Donald D. Keller

Vice President, Marketing
Jean Lin

Vice President, International Sales
Maksim Rutenberg

Vice President, Technology
Jason Dole

Director, Human Resources
Bev Ecker

Editorial

Director, New Print
Tom Evans

Managing Editor, New Print
Jeff De La Rosa

Series Editor
Nathalie Strassheim

Librarian
S. Thomas Richardson

Manager, Contracts & Compliance
(Rights & Permissions)
Loranne K. Shields

Manager, Indexing Services
David Pofelski

Digital

Director, Digital Product Development
Erika Meller

Manager, Digital Products
Jonathan Wills

Graphics and Design

Senior Art Director
Tom Evans

Senior Visual Communications Designer
Melanie Bender

Senior Web Designer/Digital Media Developer
Matthew Carrington

Media Researcher
Rosalia Bledsoe

Senior Cartographer
John M. Rejba

Manufacturing/Production

Manufacturing Manager
Anne Fritzinger

Proofreaders
Mary Kieffer
Georgina Milsted

Contents

Introduction

Are you ready for an adventure? I am! My name is Ayo. I'm an aardvark, an African mammal that eats ants and termites. I'm also a tour guide traveling the world. I hope you will come with me. We are going to explore cities around the globe. In this book, we will visit

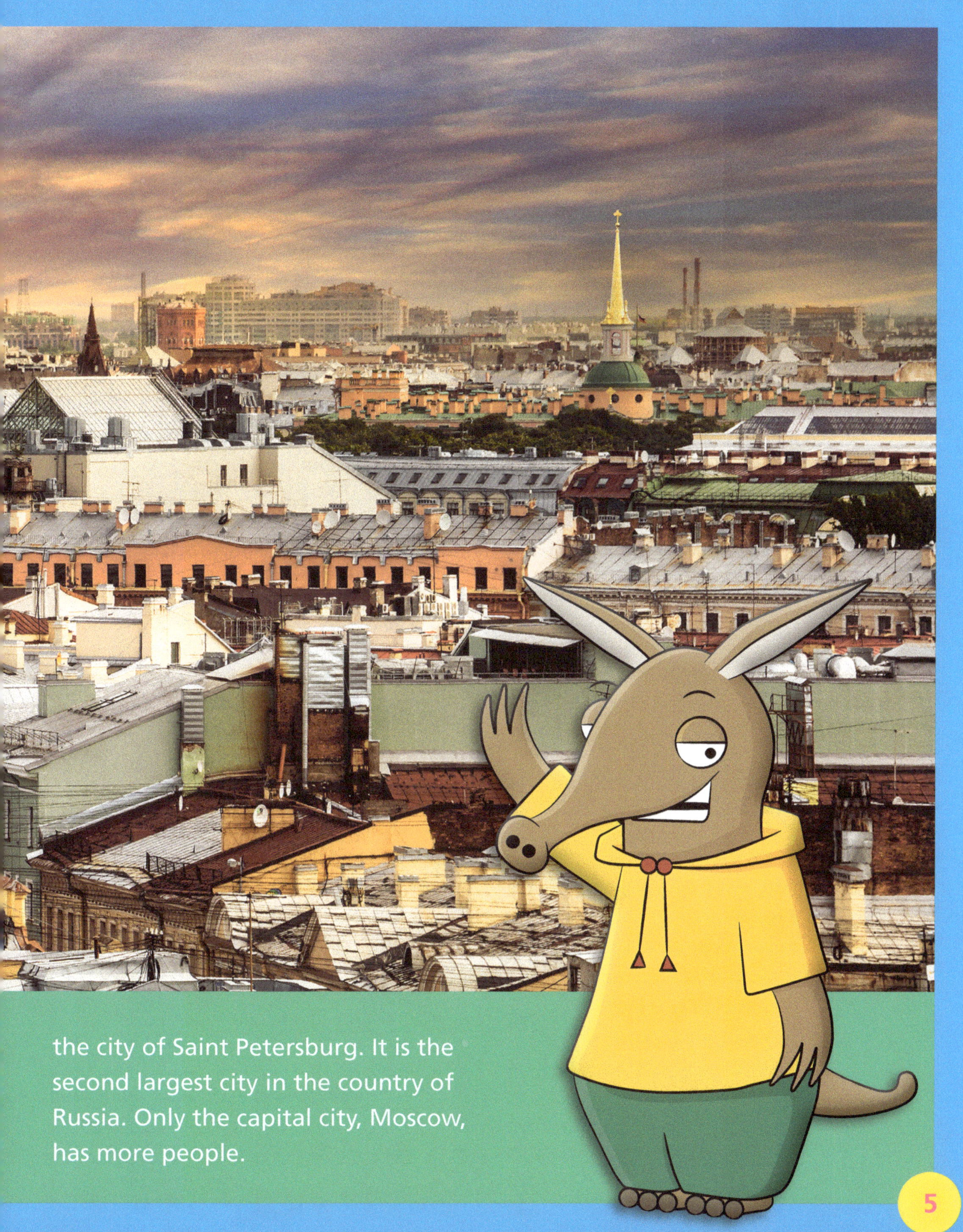

the city of Saint Petersburg. It is the second largest city in the country of Russia. Only the capital city, Moscow, has more people.

Russia is far from Africa, my home continent! Aren't you curious about my name? *Ayo* is an African word that means *joy*.

St. Petersburg is a very busy place. There are so many things to do! We won't be able to see all of it. But I think I can find the most special things for us to do. Just remember: Most people in St. Petersburg speak Russian. Many of them do not speak English at all. Some of the words may look new and strange to you. I'll try to sound them out slowly. Here's an example: One of the places we'll see on our tour is the Griboedov Canal. *Griboedov* is said like this: *GRIH boh duhv.*

We'll be talking about many things that may be new to you. If I can explain them easily, I will do so right where you are reading. If the names cannot be explained easily, or if I use them over and over again, I will put them in boldface. Boldface is type that **looks like this.** All boldface words will be defined in a glossary in the back of the book.

I hope someday you can travel with your family to St. Petersburg. You can ask to see the places we visit in this book! Then you can be the tour guide for your parents and brothers and sisters.

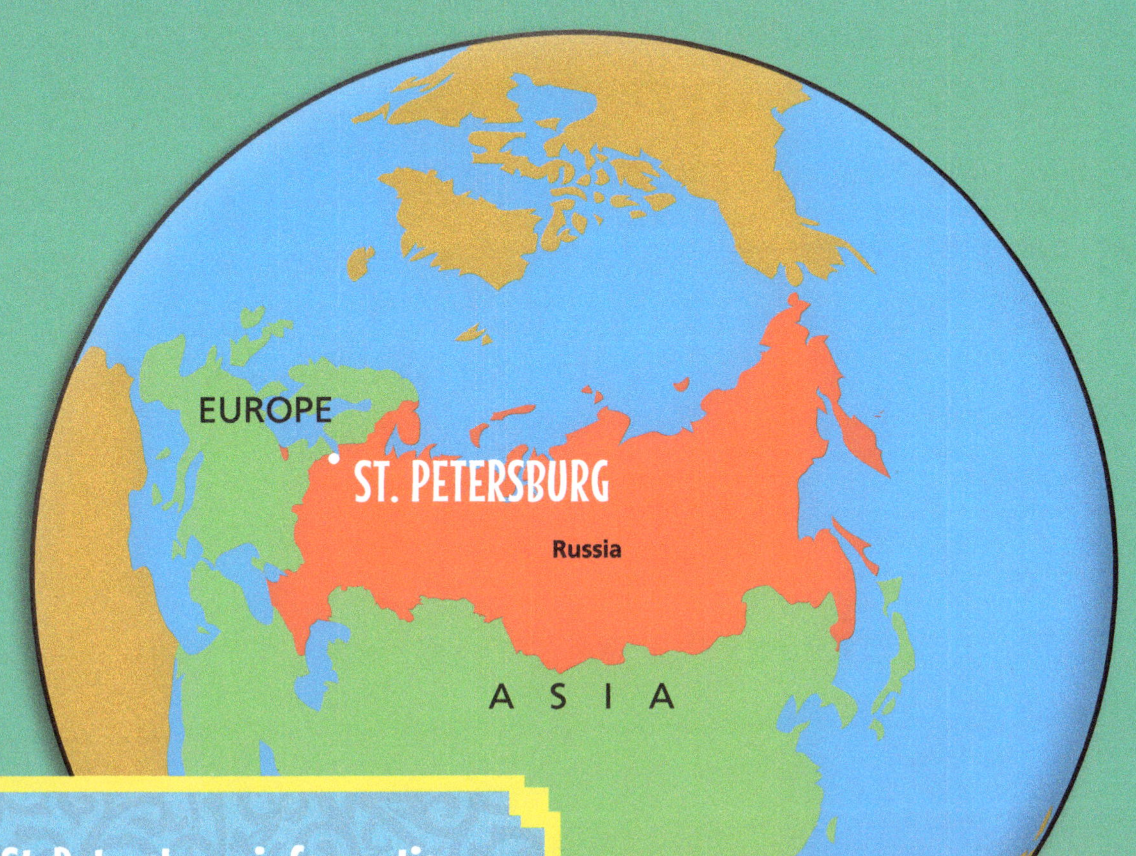

St. Petersburg information

- Population: 4,848,742

- Founded: 1703

- Need to know: St. Petersburg was the center of Russian *politics* (government) for hundreds of years. It was the capital from 1713 to 1918. Important events in the city's history include protests, revolutions, and assassinations.

- Nickname: St. Petersburg is sometimes called the *City of Bridges.* The city is built on islands. The islands are connected by hundreds of bridges.

Russia information

- Climate: Long, bitterly cold winters and mild to warm—but short—summers

- Money: Russian ruble. One hundred kopecks equal one ruble.

- Flag: The flag, adopted in 1991, was also used from 1699 to 1918.

flag of Russia

Zayachy Island

Let's start our tour where St. Petersburg began, on tiny Zayachy (*ZEYE ah kee*) Island. The Neva River flows around the island. Most of the island is taken up by the Peter and Paul Fortress. It's more than 300 years old and the oldest building in town.

How was the city started? Peter the Great was **czar** of Russia in the early 1700's. *Czar,* pronounced *zahr,* means *emperor.* Peter admired the nations of Western Europe, such as France, Great Britain, and the Netherlands. He wanted Russia to have a capital as beautiful as their great cities. A swamp was drained to make a place to build the city. The fortress was

the first building! This city has had several names since it was founded. Peter gave it a Dutch-sounding name: Sankt Piter Burkh. It soon became known as St. Petersburg. It became Petrograd at the start of World War I (1914-1918). **Communists** took control of Russia after the Russian Revolution in 1917. They named the city **Leningrad** in honor of V. I. Lenin, founder of the country's Communist party. In 1991, Communist rule ended. The city became St. Petersburg again.

Today we can bring a picnic, visit exhibits, and wait for noon, when a cannon is fired. Cover your ears!

Bridges and White Nights

Zayachy Island isn't the only island in this huge city. St. Petersburg is built on dozens of islands. Does that mean we have to travel by boat? Lucky for us, the islands are connected by bridges. Guess how many bridges there are—more than 500! Peter the Great admired other cities built right on the water, such as Venice, Italy. They served as inspiration for the new capital.

St. Petersburg is pretty far north. In winter, the sun doesn't rise until late morning. Even then, it doesn't get very bright. Then the sun sets in the middle of the afternoon! And cold? Brrrr. You really have to like cold weather to enjoy St. Petersburg in winter. We are far from my warm African home!

Summer is a different story. In late spring, the nights get lighter. Then, from June 11th to July 2nd, the sun never sets all the way. These are called the White Nights—three weeks of daylight around the clock. The streetlights don't even turn on!

We'll be walking over plenty of bridges on our visit to St. Petersburg. Here are some of my favorites:

• The Palace Bridge (see it on page 37)

• Lomonosov *(luh MAH nuh suhv)* Bridge

• Anichkov *(AN ihsh kuhv)* Bridge

The Summer Garden

Peter the Great was a very busy ruler. He fought wars, argued with the *nobility* (ruling class), and planned a new capital city. Those plans included gardens. The Summer Garden was all his idea. At first, it was designed to look like a French garden. But in 1777, most of it was destroyed by a flood. Catherine the Great, the **czarina** at the time, rebuilt it to look like an English garden.

For many years, only the nobility were allowed in the park. There is a fancy iron fence on the Neva River side of the garden. It was put there to keep the common people out! Before the Russian Revolution in 1917, we would have had to dress up to come here. Now ordinary people in comfortable clothes can enjoy the shade of the huge trees.

People and trees aren't the only things here. Let's look at some of these statues—79 in all. Many show scenes from history or *mythology* (legends). We're lucky to see them. During World War II (1939-1945), enemy bombs rained down on the city. **St. Petersburgians** protected the statues by burying them!

After the Revolution

Russia was ruled by czars
until the Russian Revolution
in 1917. Today, it is a *republic*,
a country ruled by elected
leaders. Moscow is its capital.

The Hermitage

Our next stop is the State Hermitage Museum. Most people call it the Hermitage—say HUR muh tihj. It's a great place to see art and learn some Russian history.

In front of these huge buildings, I feel tiny! The Hermitage isn't just one building. It's made up of the Small, the New, and the Great Hermitage buildings. And we can't forget the largest building—the Winter Palace. Isn't the mint green color perfect for a "winter" palace? It reminds me of mint ice cream. My favorite part of the palace is the Jordan Staircase. It leads to galleries—large rooms—full of beautiful paintings.

We can't leave without stopping at Pavilion Hall. There, we'll see the 200-year-old Peacock Clock. This clock has a mechanical peacock, owl, and chicken that all move and sing. The second hand is a dragonfly perched on a mushroom cap! All of the animals in the clock are *gilded* (covered with a thin layer of gold).

Peacock Clock

St. Isaac's Square

One of my favorite places to stand in St. Petersburg is St. Isaac's Square. No matter which way you turn, there is an amazing building to see. You can't miss St. Isaac's Cathedral. It is a huge church on the north side of the square. It is one of the world's tallest cathedrals! What makes the dome on top so shiny? It is covered in a thin layer of gold!

Across the square, on the other side of the Moyka River, is the Mariinsky *(muh RIHN skee)* Palace. **Czar** Nicholas I (1796-1855) built the Mariinsky Palace for his daughter Maria and named it after her. Nowadays, the palace holds city government offices.

On our way to the palace, we'll pass a statue of Nicholas I on horseback. Then, we'll cross the Blue Bridge, St. Petersburg's widest bridge.

Hey, look—there's another statue of a czar on a horse. This one is Peter the Great, but the statue has a nickname: the Bronze Horseman.

The Bronze Horseman

appears in a famous poem by the Russian poet Alexander Pushkin. In the poem, a young man complains to the statue about the location that Peter the Great chose for his city. The statue comes to life and chases the young man through the city.

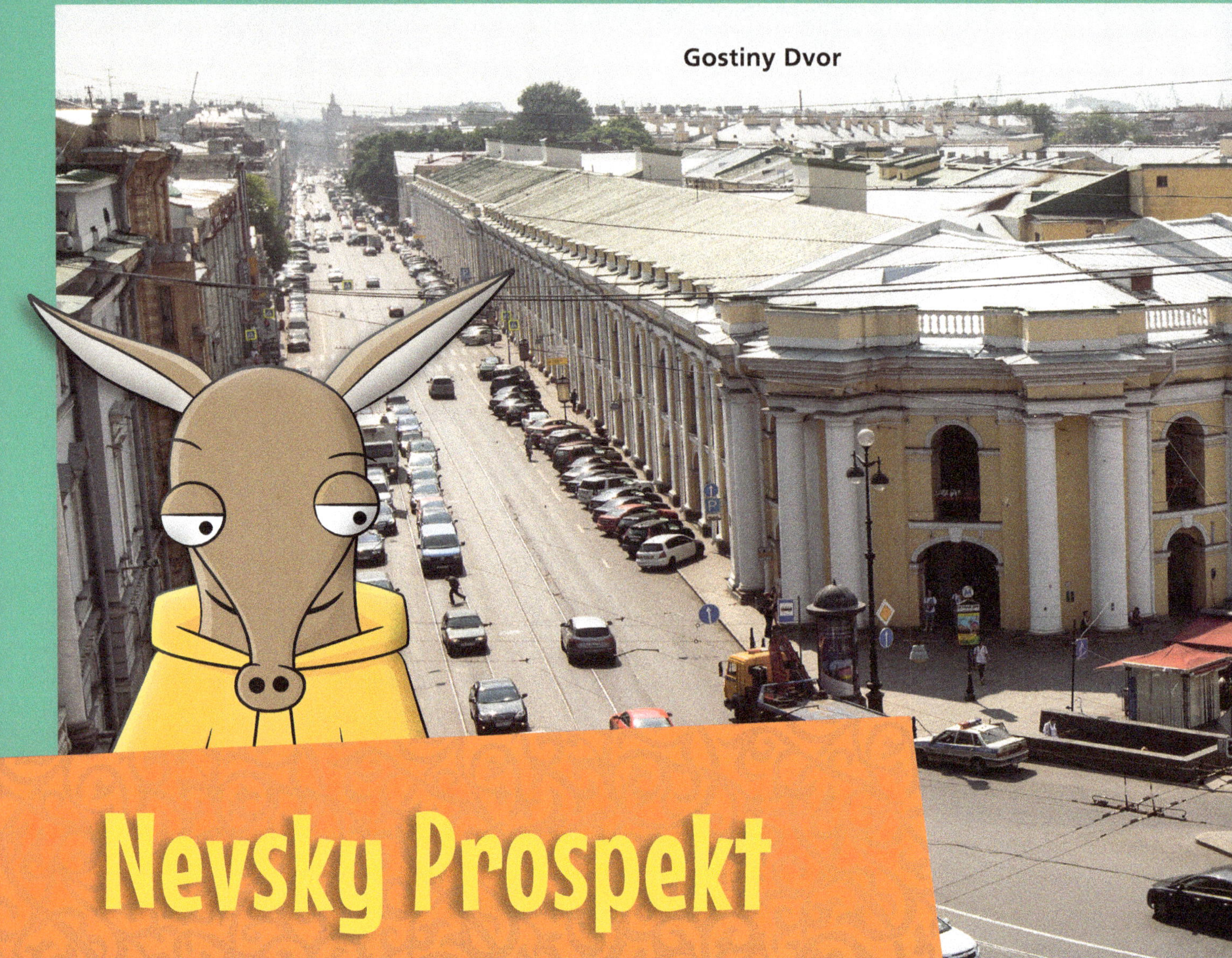

Nevsky Prospekt

Let's take a stroll along Nevsky Prospekt, St. Petersburg's main street. I want to show you a famous sign, on a building called School No. 210. I'll translate the sign for you. "Citizens!" it says. "This side of the street is more dangerous during artillery bombardment." Oh no! Do we need to worry about flying bombs? Not these days. The sign was put up long ago, when the city was **besieged** by the German army during World War II (1939-1945).

If we keep walking, we will come to the Griboedov *(GRIH boh duhv)* Canal. The Griboedov Canal winds through southwestern St. Petersburg. Tour boats load and unload passengers where Nevsky

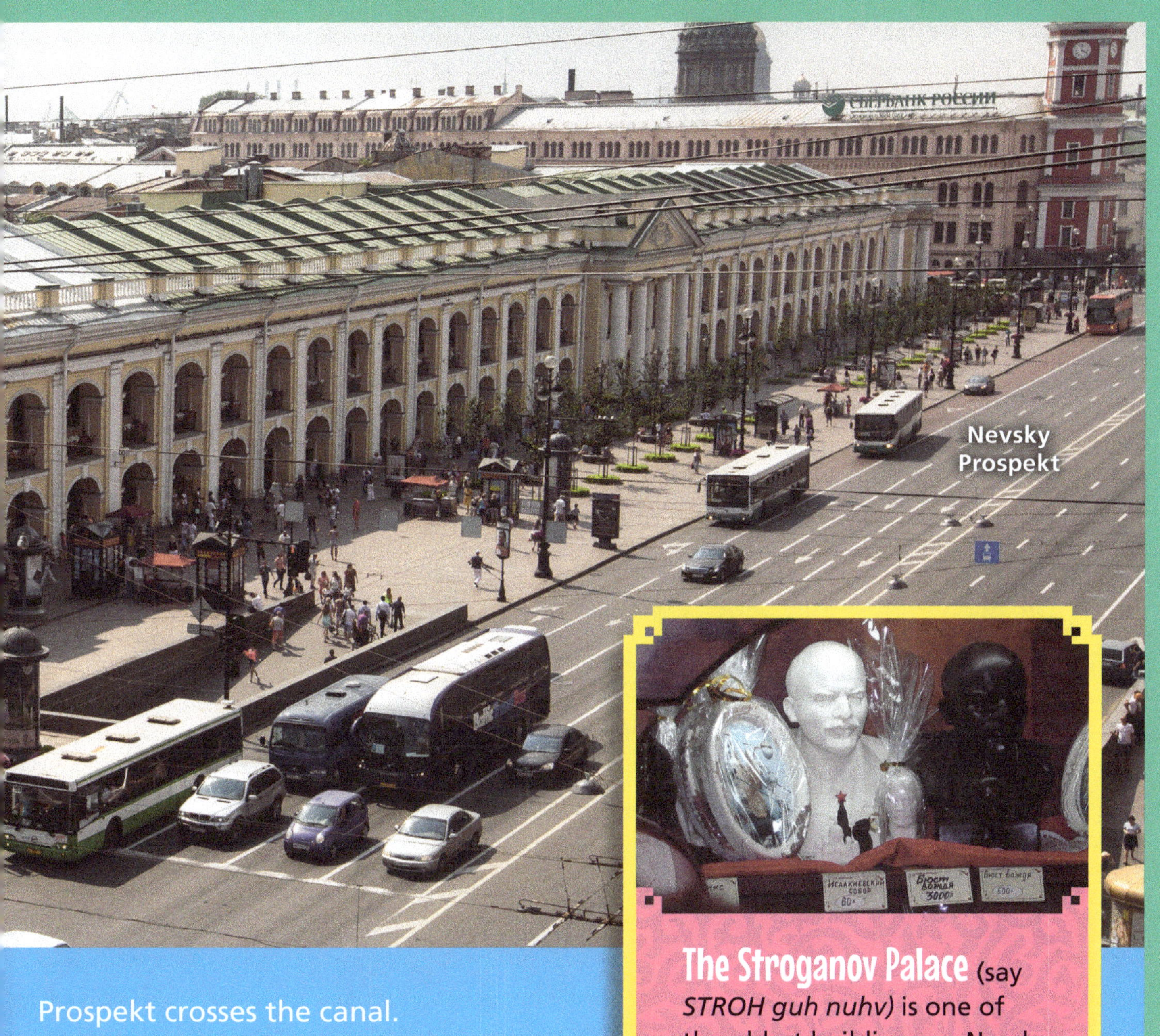

Prospekt crosses the canal.

Once we go over the canal, we're getting close to St. Petersburg's great marketplace: Gostiny Dvor *(GAH stih nee DEE vur).* It's been a busy shopping area for the last 300 years. There are markets and stores and all kinds of restaurants inside. The huge building takes up an entire city block!

The Stroganov Palace (say *STROH guh nuhv*) is one of the oldest buildings on Nevsky Prospekt. But that's not why we're stopping here. We're headed for the basement. That's where we'll find the Chocolate Museum! The chocolate they sell here is delicious, not old. You can buy a tasty chocolate sculpture. May I nibble on your **Lenin?**

Arts Square

Let's turn down a side street off Nevsky Prospekt. I'm taking you to Arts Square. It is called Arts Square because of the many theaters, museums, and other buildings nearby. As we get closer, you can see the pretty yellow Mikhailovsky *(mihk hyl UHV skee)* Palace. Inside is the Russian Museum, a great place to look at Russian art. The square and the palace were designed by the same **architect,** Carlo Rossi of Italy.

The building to the west has an unusual name— the Church of the Savior on Spilled Blood. I bet you're wondering whose blood? **Czar** Alexander II was killed on this spot in 1881. The church looks different from other large buildings around here, doesn't it? The domes look like painted onions, and there are lots of other rounded shapes. Alexander III was the son of the murdered czar. He wanted this church to be built in a traditional Russian style. Most other buildings we've seen have been built in what's called a *classical* style: straight lines, with long rows of windows and *columns* (pillars).

Just north of the Russian Museum lies the Mikhailovsky Garden. St. Petersburg's artists and deep thinkers like to spend time there. Shall we take a walk and think deeply?

Mikhailovsky Castle

Mikhailovsky Castle is a short walk from Arts Square. **Czar** Paul I became Russia's ruler in the late 1700's. He wanted a new place to live. Paul made many drawings to show **architects** how he wanted his castle. Paul had one main worry— staying safe. He asked the architects to include a *moat* (a deep ditch filled with water), a drawbridge, cannons, and secret passageways.

Paul's son Alexander became czar in the early 1800's. He did not

want to live in his father's castle. It sat empty for many years. Then it was turned into a college for army engineers. That's how the castle got its nickname—Engineer's Castle. Now it is an art museum. Some people believe the castle is haunted. There's even a short story about it, "The Ghost of the Engineer's Castle" by Nikolai Leskov. Would you like to see inside this mysterious building? We can take a tour to see the artwork on display, or we could take a tour of the castle itself.

Bolshoi Puppet Theater

St. Petersburg is a great town for theater. There's just one problem—I don't speak much Russian. I'm not sure that you do, either. Most of the best theater here is in Russian.

I know a theater we can enjoy no matter which languages we know: the Bolshoi Puppet Theater. When I say puppets, I mean hand puppets, *marionettes* (puppets moved with strings), and any other kind of puppet you can imagine. They put on all kinds of plays here, for children and for adults. Many of them are probably not like anything you've ever seen before. Let's cross the Fontanka River and walk for a few blocks to get to this special theater.

Many Bolshoi Puppet Theater shows have gone on to be performed at international theater festivals. In a city known for its beautiful old buildings, it's cool to see something new and unexpected. And I'm sure we'll have fun, even if we don't understand what the puppets are saying!

Performances at the theater include everything from Russian fairy tales to the plays of the famous English author William Shakespeare. In some shows, live actors perform with the puppets. Many shows include music and dance.

Planet Neptune Aquarium

It seems like everywhere we go in St. Petersburg, we cross water. Now let's visit creatures that live underwater, at the Planet Neptune Aquarium.

Would you like to look a shark in the eye? An underwater tunnel runs through the gigantic Main Aquarium. Sharks, moray eels, fish called groupers, and others called giant sea perches swim overhead.

There are five other *habitats* (living areas) to visit here.

Russia's North West features about 100 different types of fish from the lakes and rivers of the northwestern part of the country. My favorite is the sturgeon—that's STUR juhn. It looks a prehistoric monster.

Tropical Forests has fish from the waters of South America, Asia, Africa, and Australia. Many of these fish come from the Amazon River in South America. They include piranhas and stingrays.

Life in Caves looks like a dark cave on a Russian seacoast. Some animals here have lost the ability to see from living in the dark.

Rocky Coasts gives an up-close look at starfish, hermit crabs, and bamboo sharks.

Coral Reefs shows animals from the warm *tropics,* far away from St. Petersburg's cold northern climate. Tropics are areas close to the *equator,* the imaginary line around the center of Earth.

Grand Maket

The country of Russia is huge! It would take a long time to visit every part of it. Lucky for us, we can get a sample at the Grand Maket of Russia. The Grand Maket is a huge *scale model*—a miniature version of something big. It shows scenes of life all across Russia. There are big cities, such as St. Petersburg and Moscow; farming areas; and the cold, northern wilderness of Siberia. The Grand Maket is one of the largest scale models in the world. It's so big that we'll need to rent binoculars to see all the details.

The model even has its miniature versions of day and night. There are 13 minutes of daylight followed by 2 minutes of darkness. The parts of the model don't sit still, either. Traffic moves along roadways. Cars pass one another and stop at traffic lights. Somewhere, firefighters are putting out a fire. Somewhere else, prisoners are breaking out of jail. Railway lines crisscross the Grand Maket, and model trains run constantly.

Look for buttons to press to set parts of the model in motion. Press one and some lumberjacks cut down a tree!

Russian Railway Museum

Did you notice how many trains were in the Grand Maket? Trains must be really important in Russia. Let's visit a place that is all about trains. The Russian Railway Museum is enormous! It includes a modern building full of displays, an old *locomotive depot* (place where engines are stored), and a huge outdoor rail yard bigger than five football fields.

My favorite thing to do here is walk around the trains. We can look at more than 100 pieces of *rolling stock*—that means real train cars and locomotives. There are steam locomotives from the 1800's. There are also diesel and electric locomotives from the 1900's. We can take tours, explore exhibits, and watch videos. By the time we're done, we'll know all about the history of trains in Russia. Maybe we'll decide to become railway engineers some day.

ВПЕРЕД К КОММУНИЗМУ
СО
СО
2413

Theater Square

Let's take a long walk to Theater Square. If we go a bit out of our way, we can cross the Lions Bridge. The lion sculptures remind me of my home in Africa! They cover up the bridge supports. Look at how the cables come out of their mouths!

On the other side of the bridge, it's a short way to Theater Square. Several theaters were built here. Over the years, they burned down, or people tore them down. Finally, the grand Mariinsky Theater opened in the 1860's. Since then, famous plays and ballet dances have been put on here. Have you seen a famous ballet called the *The Nutcracker* at

Christmastime? A Russian *composer* (a person who writes music) named Peter Tchaikovsky *(cheye KUHV skee)* wrote the music for this ballet. It was first performed at the Mariinsky Theater.

Across the street is another grand building, the Rimsky-Korsakov Conservatory. Some of the most important Russian composers of classical music studied here. Outside of the conservatory are statues of two of them. On one side of the building is a statue of Mikhail Glinka. On the other side of the building is a statue of Nikolai Rimsky-Korsakov.

Vasilyevskiy Island

We'll have to cross the Neva River to reach Vasilyevskiy (say *VA sihl ee YEHV skee)* Island—the biggest of St. Petersburg's islands. Peter the Great had big plans for this place. He wanted the island to be the center of power in his new capital city. The only problem? Peter insisted that people use sailboats to get to the island and back. It would be years before there were any permanent bridges to the island.

What will we find here today? St. Petersburg University, the Academy of Sciences, and several museums make the trip worth it. There's even a floating museum on the southern **embankment.** It's the Icebreaker *Krasin.* An icebreaker is a ship that can break through thick sea ice, making a safe path for other ships. The *Krasin* was used in many Arctic expeditions and rescues. It once led *convoys* (groups) of supply ships during World War II (1939-1945). Visitors can explore the *Krasin* and learn what it was like to live and work on board.

Did you see the submarine we walked past on our way to the Icebreaker *Krasin?* The C-189 submarine was a working submarine for 35 years. I'm pretty small, but even I feel cramped inside that metal tube.

If we keep walking east, along the University **Embankment,** we'll reach the Strelka. That is the tip of the island, right across from the Winter Palace. Along the way, look left—that building seems huge, doesn't it? How far does it stretch? You're looking at the Twelve Colleges. It started out as 12 separate buildings.

They have all been connected, so the Twelve Colleges is one very long building. It's longer than three city blocks!

The embankment curves to the left, and soon we'll reach the Zoological Museum, a museum for the study of animals. I like to visit it to see the

Two major bridges connect the island to the rest of the city: the Palace Bridge and the Blagoveshchensky *(bla guhvz CHEHN skee)* Bridge. The bridges are raised every night—and stay raised about an hour to let ships pass underneath. Make sure you are on the side you want!

skeletons of mammoths. There are also a dizzying number of preserved birds and butterflies, some whales, and even dinosaurs.

When we get to the Strelka, you can't miss the two Rostral Columns. They look like towers on either side of the green *semicircle* (half circle). They used to be lighthouses guiding ships into port. Now the torches on top burn on holidays, such as the city's birthday and the New Year.

Alexander Park and Leningrad Zoo

It's just a short walk across the Birzhevoy Bridge to Alexander Park. In summer, all the trees provide plenty of shade. That seems like just the thing after a long day of exploring. But don't think we're done yet. Have you noticed the sculptures here? They look familiar…. There's the Church of the Savior on Spilled Blood! The sculptures show the famous buildings of St. Petersburg in miniature. You can see sculptures of lots of places we've seen on our tour of the city:

• Mikhailovsky Castle
• Winter Palace
• Saint Isaac's Cathedral

… to name a few. The sculptures are made of bronze.

The biggest attraction of Alexander Park is the **Leningrad** Zoo, the second biggest zoo in Russia. There are thousands of animals here from all over the world. If you feel like riding a horse, pony, or donkey, visit the Riding Circle. The Children's Zoo has farm animals, such as geese, chickens, and a cow. You can get your picture taken with a Cameroon pygmy goat as you pet and feed it. Or, get in a nice hike on the Pathfinder Track as you learn about wildlife in and around St. Petersburg.

Let's eat!

I find that kids visiting faraway places sometimes get homesick at mealtime. If that's you, don't worry. I'm sure you can find something familiar. Pizza, hot dogs, and hamburgers are never far away. But if you want to try more traditional Russian foods, here are some tips.

Winters in Russia are long and cold. Fresh fruit and vegetables used to be hard to find. Instead, Russians ate meals of bread, meat, potatoes, fish, cheese, and eggs. Shall we try two of the most popular Russian soups?

Borsch (*bohrsh*) is made from beets and served with sour cream. Shchi (*shkee*) is made from cabbage, mushrooms, and meat. Soups are often served with black bread.

Restaurants and cafes are easy to find in St. Petersburg. What else should we look for on the menu?

Pirozhki (PEER uhz kee) are pockets of dough stuffed with meat, potatoes, mushrooms, eggs, or rice. No ants or termites!

You may have tried beef Stroganoff before. It's made with beef and sour cream and served over noodles.

Thin pancakes called *blini (BLIHN ee)* are my favorite. They're usually topped with butter, jam, or sour cream. Some people top them with caviar—that's fish eggs!

Getting around

Many things in Russia are big, aren't they? Peter the Great's plans, St. Petersburg's palaces, the Rostral Columns, the country itself—they all seem enormous, especially to little aardvarks! How do Russians get around their large country? The Grand Maket and Russian Railway Museum gave you a clue: trains!

St. Petersburg has four main train stations:

• Moscow Station: trains to Moscow as well as central, southern, and eastern Russia

an underground Metro station

St. Petersburgians call their subway the Metro. It runs deep underground and connects to the four main train depots. Metro riders zip between 67 beautifully decorated stations.

- Vitebsk Station: trains to such countries as Estonia, Latvia, Lithuania, Belarus, Ukraine, and Moldova

- Finland Station: the express train to Helsinki, Finland

- Ladoga Station is St. Petersburg's newest train station. Trains run to the same places as those from Moscow Station.

Does the city seem too big to see on foot? Let's put those waterways to work before we finish up our tour. Boat cruises are a fun way to see St. Petersburg. They run along the Neva, Fontanka, and Moyka rivers and the Griboedov Canal. Board a boat where Nevsky Prospekt crosses a canal or river.

Gostiny Dvor
Summer Garden
Peacock Clock
Church of the Savior on Spilled Blood

Icebreaker Krasin
Thanks for exploring
St. Petersburg with
me. I hope to see
you soon!

Ayo

Glossary

architect *(AHR kuh tehkt)* A person who designs buildings

besiege *(buh SEEJ)* To surround a city or fortress and cut it off from supplies, trying to capture it

Communism *(KOM yuh nihz uhm)*, **Communist party** A system of government control of land and wealth. The Communist Party ruled Russia from 1917 to 1991.

czar, czarina *(zahr, zahr EE nuh)* A Russian word for emperor or empress

embankment *(ehm BANGK muhnt)* A raised bank of earth or stones used to hold back water or support a roadway

Leningrad *(LEHN ihn grahd)* St. Petersburg's name between 1924 and 1991. It was named after V. I. Lenin (1870-1924). He founded the Soviet Communist Party. It ruled Russia from 1917 to 1991.

St. Petersburgian *(saynt PEE tuhrz BUHRG ee uhn)* A person who lives in St. Petersburg

Acknowledgments

Cover © Baturina Yuliya, Shutterstock
Ayo artwork by Matthew Carrington

4-7   © Shutterstock
8-9   © Leonid Plotnikov, Shutterstock; *Peter the Great, Tzar of Russia* (1698), oil on canvas by Godfrey Kneller; British Museum
10-17   © Shutterstock
18-19   © Shutterstock; Jennifer Boyer (licensed under CC BY 2.0)
20-23   © Shutterstock
24-25   © Russ Images/Alamy Images
26-27   © SPUTNIK/Alamy Images; © Vladimir Wrangel, Shutterstock
28-29   © Andrey Picard, Shutterstock; © Andrey Armyagov, Shutterstock
30-31   © Alexander Demianchuk, Getty Images
32-37   © Shutterstock
38-39   © Shutterstock; © ITAR-TASS Photo Agency/Alamy Images
40-41   © John Kellerman, Alamy Images; © Tatiana Volgutova, Shutterstock; © Denis Belyaevskiy, Shutterstock; © Brent Hofacker, Shutterstock; © Tatyana Berkovich, iStockphoto
42-43   © Moomusician/Shutterstock; © Roman Evgenev, Shutterstock

Index

For further reading

Books

Mahony, Sandy and Mary Lou Brown, *Ivan's Voyage to St. Petersburg, Russia.* CreateSpace Independent Publishing Platform, 2016.

Stanley, Diane, *Peter the Great.* HarperCollins, 1999.

Whelan, Gloria, *Angel on the Square.* HarperCollins, 2003.

Websites

Fun facts to know about St. Petersburg
https://friendlylocalguides.com/blog/50-facts-about-st-petersburg

Guide to visiting less-well-known places in St. Petersburg
http://www.atlasobscura.com/things-to-do/saint-petersburg-russia

More fun things for kids to do in St. Petersburg
https://travelforkids.com/Funtodo/Russia/stpetersburg.htm

Visiting the Hermitage
https://www.hermitagemuseum.org/wps/portal/hermitage/?lng=en